I0005125

Beyond Basic SQL: Advanced Query Strategies for SQL Server Experts ®

About the Author

George N. Makridis: George is a 30-year veteran of the computer industry, he has developed thousands of lines of code. He lectures internationally on databases and runs a YouTube channel. For the latest news on George's activities, check out his online courses. You can contact George at george@sqlwithgeorge.com.

Dedication

This book is dedicated to the many teachers, authors, coworkers, friends, students, and online posters who have helped expand my computer knowledge over these many years.

"The way of a fool is right in his own eyes, but a wise man listens to advice." - Proverbs 12:15 (ESV)

-Richard Blum

Authot's note

While every effort has been made to keep spacing equal in all circumstances, it is not possible to keep all code examples inside the boxes in one piece and not span across pages. This alone makes pagination difficult and is the reason why white spaces are introduced in places where it normally should be occupied with text.

Where to Go from Here

Every effort has been made to explain the contents in this book and examples where provided where possible.

If you need go further than this very book, there are a few ways of doing so:

- Getting in contact with the author, George Makridis at george@sqlwithgeorge.com
- Visiting the YouTube channel SQL with George - YouTube where videos might be able to further cover your thirst for knowledge
- George is also giving courses on well-known courses platforms
- Finally, one on one sessions can be arranged to explain your issues in a private session. This can be arranged by contacting George in the above email address.

Chapter 0: Introduction - Beyond Basic SQL – Elevating Query Mastery

SQL is the foundation of data retrieval, but mastering its advanced capabilities separates skilled developers from true SQL Server experts. *Beyond Basic SQL: Advanced Query Strategies for SQL Server Experts* is designed to bridge the gap between fundamental SQL knowledge and expert-level query optimization. This book is crafted for database professionals, developers, and analysts seeking to write high-performance, scalable, and maintainable SQL queries.

The journey begins with **query performance fundamentals**, covering execution plans, bottleneck identification, and indexing strategies to fine-tune database efficiency. As the chapters progress, the book dives into **complex joins, set operations, and window functions**, empowering readers to perform sophisticated data manipulations. Further, it explores **subqueries, Common Table Expressions (CTEs), and dynamic SQL**, providing techniques for writing flexible and efficient queries.

Beyond query writing, the book tackles **transaction management, concurrency control, and performance tuning**, equipping readers with strategies to handle high-concurrency environments effectively. The final chapters focus on **temporary tables, derived tables, and profiling tools**, ensuring readers can analyze and optimize query execution. The book concludes with **best practices for scalable SQL**, ensuring queries remain efficient as datasets grow.

By mastering the concepts in this book, readers will be equipped to tackle real-world SQL challenges, optimize complex queries, and enhance the performance of SQL Server databases in high-demand environments.

Chapter 1: Optimizing Query Performance – Foundations of High-Speed SQL

1.1 Introduction

Optimizing query performance is essential for managing large-scale databases efficiently. Poorly written queries can lead to slow response times, increased server load, and inefficient use of resources. This chapter covers **execution plans, performance bottlenecks, and best practices for writing high-performance SQL queries** in SQL Server.

1.2 Understanding Execution Plans and How to Read Them

SQL Server provides **execution plans** to show how a query is executed internally. These plans help identify inefficiencies such as table scans, missing indexes, and suboptimal join strategies.

1.2.1 How to Generate an Execution Plan

Execution plans can be obtained using:

- **SSMS GUI**: Click on "Display Estimated Execution Plan" (Ctrl + L) or "Include Actual Execution Plan" (Ctrl + M).
- **T-SQL Command**:

```
SET STATISTICS IO ON;
SET STATISTICS TIME ON;
GO
SELECT * FROM Orders WHERE OrderDate > '2023-01-01';
GO
SET STATISTICS IO OFF;
SET STATISTICS TIME OFF;
```

- **EXPLAIN using SHOWPLAN_XML**:

```
SET SHOWPLAN_XML ON;
GO
SELECT * FROM Orders WHERE OrderDate > '2023-01-01';
GO
SET SHOWPLAN_XML OFF;
```

1.2.2 Key Elements of an Execution Plan

1. **Table Scan vs. Index Seek**
   - **Table Scan**: The entire table is read, leading to slow performance.

- o **Index Seek**: Uses an index to locate rows efficiently.

Example: Avoiding a Table Scan

```
SELECT * FROM Orders WHERE OrderDate > '2023-01-01';
```

- o If OrderDate is **not indexed**, SQL Server will do a **table scan**.

- o Adding an index speeds up filtering:

```
CREATE INDEX IX_Orders_OrderDate ON Orders(OrderDate);
```

2. **Join Types**

- o **Nested Loop Join**: Efficient for small datasets.

- o **Merge Join**: Used when both tables are sorted.

- o **Hash Join**: Used for large, unsorted datasets.

Example: Using an Indexed Join Instead of a Hash Join

```
SELECT c.CustomerName, o.OrderTotal
FROM Customers c
JOIN Orders o ON c.CustomerID = o.CustomerID
WHERE o.OrderDate > '2023-01-01';
```

- o Without an index on Orders.CustomerID, SQL Server might perform a **hash join**.

- o Adding an index converts it to a **nested loop join**:

```
CREATE INDEX IX_Orders_CustomerID ON Orders(CustomerID);
```

3. **Estimated vs. Actual Execution Plan**

- o **Estimated Execution Plan:** Shows SQL Server's prediction of query execution.

- o **Actual Execution Plan:** Includes real execution statistics (e.g., actual rows returned).

Example: Generating an Actual Execution Plan

```
SET STATISTICS IO, TIME ON;
SELECT * FROM Orders WHERE CustomerID = 101;
SET STATISTICS IO, TIME OFF;
```

1.3 Identifying Performance Bottlenecks in Queries

1.3.1 Detecting Slow Queries

SQL Server provides tools for detecting slow queries:

- **Query Store** (sys.query_store_runtime_stats)

- **Dynamic Management Views (DMVs)**

- **SQL Server Profiler and Extended Events**

Example: Finding the Most Expensive Queries

```
SELECT TOP 5 total_worker_time/execution_count AS Avg_CPU_Time,
       total_logical_reads/execution_count AS Avg_Reads,
       execution_count,
       text AS Query_Text
FROM sys.dm_exec_query_stats
CROSS APPLY sys.dm_exec_sql_text(sql_handle)
ORDER BY Avg_CPU_Time DESC;
```

1.3.2 Common Causes of Slow Queries and Solutions

Issue	Cause	Solution
Full Table Scans	No index or incorrect indexing	Add a covering index (INCLUDE columns)
Blocking & Deadlocks	Transactions holding locks for too long	Optimize transaction scope
Excessive Joins	Too many unnecessary joins	Remove redundant joins, use indexed joins
Sorting Overhead	ORDER BY without indexes	Create an index on the ORDER BY column
Excessive Temporary Tables	Too many temp tables in queries	Use CTEs or indexed tables instead

1.4 Best Practices for Writing Efficient SQL Queries

1.4.1 Avoiding SELECT *

Using SELECT * increases I/O and slows performance.

Bad Query (SELECT *)

```
SELECT * FROM Orders WHERE OrderDate > '2023-01-01';
```

Optimized Query (Selecting Only Necessary Columns)

```
SELECT OrderID, CustomerID, OrderTotal FROM Orders WHERE OrderDate >
'2023-01-01';
```

1.4.2 Using EXISTS Instead of IN

EXISTS is faster than IN for large datasets.

Bad Query (Using IN)

```
SELECT * FROM Customers WHERE CustomerID IN (SELECT CustomerID FROM
Orders);
```

Optimized Query (Using EXISTS)

```
SELECT * FROM Customers c WHERE EXISTS (SELECT 1 FROM Orders o WHERE
o.CustomerID = c.CustomerID);
```

1.4.3 Indexing WHERE and JOIN Conditions

Indexes should be used on frequently filtered and joined columns.

Example: Creating an Index for JOIN Conditions

```
CREATE INDEX IX_Orders_CustomerID ON Orders(CustomerID);
```

1.4.4 Using Proper Data Types

Mismatched data types lead to implicit conversions, slowing performance.

Bad Query (Implicit Conversion)

```
SELECT * FROM Orders WHERE OrderDate = '2023-01-01';
```

Optimized Query (Explicit Conversion)

```
SELECT * FROM Orders WHERE OrderDate = CONVERT(DATE, '2023-01-01');
```

1.4.5 Optimizing Pagination

Pagination should avoid skipping large numbers of rows.

Bad Query (Slow Pagination Using OFFSET)

```
SELECT * FROM Orders ORDER BY OrderDate OFFSET 50000 ROWS FETCH NEXT
100 ROWS ONLY;
```

Optimized Query (Using an Indexed Key for Pagination)

```
SELECT * FROM Orders WHERE OrderID > 50000 ORDER BY OrderID FETCH NEXT
100 ROWS ONLY;
```

1.5 Summary

- **Execution plans** help identify inefficient query patterns.

- **Table scans, missing indexes, and inefficient joins** are major performance bottlenecks.

- **Best practices** include avoiding SELECT *, using EXISTS over IN, proper indexing, and optimizing pagination.

- **Regularly monitoring query performance** with Query Store and DMVs ensures long-term efficiency.

By following these principles, SQL queries can be optimized for **speed, efficiency, and scalability,** ensuring a well-performing SQL Server database.

Chapter 2: Mastering Indexing: Boosting Query Speed

2.1 Introduction

Efficient indexing is critical for query optimization in SQL Server. Well-designed indexes can significantly reduce execution time, while poor indexing can lead to performance bottlenecks. This chapter explores different index types, covering indexes, filtered indexes, and indexing strategies for complex queries.

2.2 Clustered vs. Non-Clustered Indexes

2.2.1 Understanding Clustered Indexes

A **clustered index** determines the physical order of data in a table. Each table can have only <u>one</u> clustered index, typically on the **primary key**.

Example: Creating a Clustered Index on the Primary Key

```
CREATE CLUSTERED INDEX IX_Customers_CustomerID
ON Customers(CustomerID);
```

Benefits:

- Faster retrieval for range queries.
- Efficient sorting and ordering.

Limitations<u>:</u>

- Only one per table.
- Insert-heavy tables may experience fragmentation.

Example: Efficient Range Query with Clustered Index

```
SELECT * FROM Orders WHERE OrderDate BETWEEN '2023-01-01' AND '2023-12-31';
```

Since OrderDate is **indexed**, SQL Server can use an **index seek** instead of scanning all rows.

2.2.2 Understanding Non-Clustered Indexes

A **non-clustered index** creates a separate structure from the table data, storing pointers to the actual rows.

Example: Creating a Non-Clustered Index

```
CREATE NONCLUSTERED INDEX IX_Orders_CustomerID
ON Orders(CustomerID);
```

Benefits:

- Multiple non-clustered indexes per table.
- Speeds up queries filtering on indexed columns.

Limitations:

- Additional storage required.
- Requires maintenance on inserts, updates, and deletes.

Example: Query Optimization with Non-Clustered Index

```
SELECT OrderID, OrderTotal FROM Orders WHERE CustomerID = 101;
```

With an index on CustomerID, SQL Server can efficiently **seek** instead of scanning all rows.

2.3 Covering Indexes and Filtered Indexes

2.3.1 Covering Indexes

A **covering index** contains all the columns needed for a query, reducing the need for additional lookups.

Example: Creating a Covering Index

```
CREATE NONCLUSTERED INDEX IX_Orders_Covering
ON Orders(CustomerID)
INCLUDE (OrderTotal, OrderDate);
```

Why?

- **Includes** OrderTotal and OrderDate, eliminating lookups in the base table.
- **Speeds up queries** that only need these columns.

Example: Query Using the Covering Index

```
SELECT CustomerID, OrderTotal, OrderDate
FROM Orders WHERE CustomerID = 200;
```

SQL Server retrieves data **entirely from the index**, avoiding extra lookups.

2.3.2 Filtered Indexes

A **filtered index** improves performance by indexing only a subset of data.

Example: Creating a Filtered Index

```
CREATE NONCLUSTERED INDEX IX_Orders_Active
ON Orders(OrderStatus)
WHERE OrderStatus = 'Shipped';
```

Why?

- Reduces index size.

- Speeds up queries that filter on OrderStatus = 'Shipped'.

Example: Query Using the Filtered Index

```
SELECT OrderID, OrderDate FROM Orders WHERE OrderStatus = 'Shipped';
```

SQL Server **skips irrelevant rows**, making the query much faster.

2.4 Indexing Strategies for Complex Queries

2.4.1 Multi-Column Indexing

When filtering on multiple columns, a **composite index** improves efficiency.

Example: Creating a Multi-Column Index

```
CREATE NONCLUSTERED INDEX IX_Orders_CustomerDate
ON Orders(CustomerID, OrderDate);
```

Best Practices:

- **Order matters:** The first column should be the most frequently filtered.

- Queries filtering **only on the second column** won't fully benefit.

Example: Query Optimized with Multi-Column Index

```
SELECT OrderID FROM Orders WHERE CustomerID = 101 AND OrderDate >
'2023-01-01';
```

This index speeds up queries that filter **both** CustomerID and OrderDate.

2.4.2 Indexed Joins

Joins are faster when foreign keys have **non-clustered indexes**.

Example: Indexing for Faster Joins

```
CREATE NONCLUSTERED INDEX IX_Orders_CustomerID ON Orders(CustomerID);
```

Example: Optimized Join Query

```
SELECT c.CustomerName, o.OrderTotal
FROM Customers c
JOIN Orders o ON c.CustomerID = o.CustomerID
WHERE o.OrderDate > '2023-01-01';
```

Why?

- The **index on Orders.CustomerID** speeds up the join.
- SQL Server can use an **index seek** instead of a scan.

Joins are faster when foreign keys have **non-clustered indexes**.

Example: Indexing for Faster Joins

```
CREATE NONCLUSTERED INDEX IX_Orders_CustomerID ON Orders(CustomerID);
```

Example: Optimized Join Query

```
SELECT c.CustomerName, o.OrderTotal
FROM Customers c
JOIN Orders o ON c.CustomerID = o.CustomerID
WHERE o.OrderDate > '2023-01-01';
```

Why?

- The **index on Orders.CustomerID** speeds up the join.
- SQL Server can use an **index seek** instead of a scan.

2.4.3 Avoiding Index Overhead

Too many indexes **slow down inserts and updates**.

Example: Balancing Indexes

Instead of indexing every column separately:

```
CREATE NONCLUSTERED INDEX IX_Orders_Optimized
ON Orders(CustomerID, OrderDate) INCLUDE (OrderTotal);
```

This single index helps **multiple queries** without excessive overhead.

2.5 Summary

- **Clustered indexes** improve range queries by sorting data physically.
- **Non-clustered indexes** speed up lookups but require additional storage.
- **Covering indexes** prevent extra lookups, improving query performance.
- **Filtered indexes** target specific subsets of data for optimization.
- **Multi-column indexes and indexed joins** enhance complex queries.
- **Avoid over-indexing** to prevent performance degradation on inserts and updates.

By mastering indexing strategies, you can **dramatically improve SQL query performance** while maintaining an optimal database structure.

Chapter 3: Advanced Joins and Set Operations

3.1 Inner, Outer, Cross, and Self Joins Deep Dive

3.1.1 Inner Join

An **INNER JOIN** returns only matching rows between two tables.

Example: Inner Join

```
SELECT c.CustomerID, c.CustomerName, o.OrderID, o.OrderDate
FROM Customers c
INNER JOIN Orders o ON c.CustomerID = o.CustomerID;
```

- Retrieves customers who have placed orders.
- Rows without a match in either table are excluded.

3.1.2 Outer Joins (LEFT, RIGHT, FULL)

Returns all rows from the left table and matching rows from the right table; unmatched right-side rows return NULL.

Left Join Example

```
SELECT c.CustomerID, c.CustomerName, o.OrderID, o.OrderDate
FROM Customers c
LEFT JOIN Orders o ON c.CustomerID = o.CustomerID;
```

Includes customers who haven't placed orders.

Right Join Example

Similar to LEFT JOIN but returns all records from the right table.

```
SELECT c.CustomerID, c.CustomerName, o.OrderID, o.OrderDate
FROM Customers c
RIGHT JOIN Orders o ON c.CustomerID = o.CustomerID;
```

Ensures all orders are listed, even if they don't have associated customers.

Full Outer Join Example

Combines LEFT and RIGHT JOINs, including all unmatched rows from both tables.

```
SELECT c.CustomerID, c.CustomerName, o.OrderID, o.OrderDate
FROM Customers c
FULL OUTER JOIN Orders o ON c.CustomerID = o.CustomerID;
```

Retrieves all customers and orders, even those without matches.

3.1.3 Cross Join

A **CROSS JOIN** returns the Cartesian product of both tables (every row in Table A joins with every row in Table B).

```
SELECT c.CustomerName, p.ProductName
FROM Customers c
CROSS JOIN Products p;
```

Useful for generating all possible combinations.

3.1.4 Self Join

A **SELF JOIN** joins a table with itself to compare related records.

```
SELECT e1.EmployeeID, e1.EmployeeName, e2.EmployeeName AS ManagerName
FROM Employees e1
INNER JOIN Employees e2 ON e1.ManagerID = e2.EmployeeID;
```

Retrieves employees with their respective managers.

3.2 Using APPLY (CROSS APPLY & OUTER APPLY) Effectively

APPLY is used to join a table with a table-valued function or subquery.

CROSS APPLY Example

Returns only rows where the function/subquery produces results.

```
SELECT c.CustomerID, c.CustomerName, o.*
FROM Customers c
CROSS APPLY (
    SELECT TOP 3 OrderID, OrderDate, TotalAmount
    FROM Orders o
    WHERE o.CustomerID = c.CustomerID
    ORDER BY OrderDate DESC
) o;
```

Fetches the latest 3 orders per customer.

OUTER APPLY Example

Includes customers even if they have no orders.

```
SELECT c.CustomerID, c.CustomerName, o.*
FROM Customers c
OUTER APPLY (
    SELECT TOP 3 OrderID, OrderDate, TotalAmount
    FROM Orders o
    WHERE o.CustomerID = c.CustomerID
    ORDER BY OrderDate DESC
) o;
```

Similar to CROSS APPLY but ensures all customers appear, even if they have no orders.

3.3 UNION, INTERSECT, and EXCEPT for Advanced Data Retrieval

3.3.1 UNION & UNION ALL

UNION combines result sets, removing duplicates, while **UNION ALL** keeps all records.

UNION Example (Removing Duplicates)

```
SELECT CustomerID, CustomerName FROM Customers
UNION
SELECT SupplierID, SupplierName FROM Suppliers;
```

Combines customer and supplier lists without duplicates.

UNION ALL Example (Keeping Duplicates)

```
SELECT CustomerID, CustomerName FROM Customers
UNION ALL
SELECT SupplierID, SupplierName FROM Suppliers;
```

Preserves duplicates.

3.3.2 INTERSECT (Finding Common Records)

INTERSECT returns only common records between two queries.

```
SELECT CustomerID, CustomerName FROM Customers
INTERSECT
SELECT CustomerID, CustomerName FROM VIP_Customers;
```

Retrieves customers who are also VIP customers.

3.3.3 EXCEPT (Finding Differences)

EXCEPT returns records from the first query that aren't in the second query.

```
SELECT CustomerID, CustomerName FROM Customers
EXCEPT
SELECT CustomerID, CustomerName FROM VIP_Customers;
```

Lists customers who are **not** VIPs.

3.4 Summary

- **Joins** help combine tables: INNER (matches), OUTER (partial matches), CROSS (Cartesian), and SELF (table joins itself).

- **APPLY** is useful for subqueries, where CROSS APPLY filters and OUTER APPLY includes unmatched rows.

- **Set operations** (UNION, INTERSECT, EXCEPT) help with advanced data retrieval.

Chapter 4: Working with Window Functions for Analytics

4.1 Introduction to Window Functions

Window functions allow calculations across a set of table rows related to the current row, without collapsing data into a single output row (unlike GROUP BY).

4.1.1 Syntax of Window Functions

```
function_name() OVER (
    [PARTITION BY column]
    [ORDER BY column]
    [ROWS or RANGE clause]
)
```

- PARTITION BY groups rows into subsets.
- ORDER BY determines processing order within partitions.
- ROWS or RANGE defines a frame of rows for calculations.

4.2 Using OVER(), PARTITION BY, and ORDER BY

4.2.1 OVER() Without PARTITION BY

Applying aggregate functions without collapsing rows.

```
SELECT EmployeeID, EmployeeName, Salary,
       AVG(Salary) OVER () AS AvgSalary
FROM Employees;
```

Returns the average salary across **all rows** without grouping.

4.2.2 PARTITION BY Example

Divides data into logical groups before applying a function.

```
SELECT EmployeeID, DepartmentID, EmployeeName, Salary,
       AVG(Salary) OVER (PARTITION BY DepartmentID) AS AvgDeptSalary
FROM Employees;
```

Computes the **average salary per department** without losing row-level detail.

4.2.3 ORDER BY Within OVER()

Used for ranking and cumulative functions.

```
SELECT EmployeeID, EmployeeName, Salary,
       SUM(Salary) OVER (ORDER BY Salary) AS RunningTotal
FROM Employees;
```

Generates a running total of salaries.

4.3 ROW_NUMBER(), RANK(), DENSE_RANK(), and NTILE()

4.3.1 ROW_NUMBER()

Assigns a unique row number within each partition.

```
SELECT EmployeeID, DepartmentID, EmployeeName, Salary,
       ROW_NUMBER() OVER (PARTITION BY DepartmentID ORDER BY Salary
DESC) AS RowNum   .
FROM Employees;
```

Ranks employees **by salary within each department**, with **no gaps**.

4.3.2 RANK()

Similar to ROW_NUMBER(), but assigns the same rank to **ties**, creating gaps.

```
SELECT EmployeeID, DepartmentID, EmployeeName, Salary,
       RANK() OVER (PARTITION BY DepartmentID ORDER BY Salary DESC) AS
Rank
FROM Employees;
```

Employees with the same salary get the same rank, but **skips numbers** for ties.

4.3.3 DENSE_RANK()

Like RANK(), but **doesn't skip ranks** after ties.

```
SELECT EmployeeID, DepartmentID, EmployeeName, Salary,
       DENSE_RANK() OVER (PARTITION BY DepartmentID ORDER BY Salary
DESC) AS DenseRank
FROM Employees;
```

Ensures ranking remains sequential, even when ties exist.

4.3.4 NTILE()

Divides results into **N equal groups**.

```
SELECT EmployeeID, EmployeeName, Salary,
       NTILE(4) OVER (ORDER BY Salary DESC) AS Quartile
FROM Employees;
```

Splits employees into **4 salary quartiles** (top 25%, next 25%, etc.).

4.4 Advanced Aggregate Functions with Windowing

4.4.1 Running Totals Using SUM()

```
SELECT EmployeeID, EmployeeName, Salary,
       SUM(Salary) OVER (PARTITION BY DepartmentID ORDER BY Salary) AS
RunningTotal
FROM Employees;
```

Computes **cumulative salary** within each department.

4.4.2 Moving Averages with ROWS BETWEEN

```
SELECT EmployeeID, EmployeeName, Salary,
       AVG(Salary) OVER (ORDER BY EmployeeID ROWS BETWEEN 2 PRECEDING
AND CURRENT ROW) AS MovingAvg
FROM Employees;
```

Computes **3-row moving average** of salaries.

4.4.3 FIRST_VALUE() and LAST_VALUE()

```
SELECT EmployeeID, EmployeeName, Salary,
       FIRST_VALUE(EmployeeName) OVER (PARTITION BY DepartmentID ORDER
BY Salary DESC) AS HighestPaid
FROM Employees;
```

Finds the **highest-paid employee** per department.

4.5 Summary

- **OVER()** enables windowing calculations without collapsing data.

- **PARTITION BY** segments data before applying functions.

- **Ranking functions** (ROW_NUMBER, RANK, DENSE_RANK, NTILE) help with analytics.

- **Advanced aggregates** like running totals and moving averages provide deep insights.

Chapter 5: Writing Efficient Subqueries and Common Table Expressions (CTEs)

5.1 Introduction to Subqueries and CTEs

Subqueries and **Common Table Expressions (CTEs)** allow complex queries to be broken into manageable parts. However, inefficient usage can lead to performance bottlenecks.

5.2 Optimizing Correlated Subqueries

A **correlated subquery** runs once for each row in the outer query, making it inefficient if not optimized properly.

5.2.1 Basic Correlated Subquery Example

```
SELECT e.EmployeeID, e.EmployeeName, e.Salary,
       (SELECT AVG(Salary)
         FROM Employees
         WHERE DepartmentID = e.DepartmentID) AS AvgDeptSalary
FROM Employees e;
```

- Computes the **average salary per department** for each employee.
- The subquery executes **once per row**, leading to **performance issues** in large datasets.

5.2.2 Optimizing with JOIN Instead of Correlated Subquery

Using **JOIN** instead of a correlated subquery improves performance.

```
SELECT e.EmployeeID, e.EmployeeName, e.Salary, d.AvgDeptSalary
FROM Employees e
JOIN (SELECT DepartmentID, AVG(Salary) AS AvgDeptSalary
       FROM Employees
       GROUP BY DepartmentID) d
ON e.DepartmentID = d.DepartmentID;
```

Precomputes the **average salary per department** before joining, improving efficiency.

5.2.3 EXISTS vs. IN for Subquery Optimization

Using EXISTS is often more efficient than IN, especially when checking large datasets.

Using IN (Less Efficient for Large Datasets)

```
SELECT EmployeeID, EmployeeName
FROM Employees
WHERE DepartmentID IN (SELECT DepartmentID FROM Departments WHERE
Location = 'New York');
```

Using EXISTS (More Efficient for Large Datasets)

```
SELECT EmployeeID, EmployeeName
FROM Employees e
WHERE EXISTS (SELECT 1 FROM Departments d WHERE d.DepartmentID =
e.DepartmentID AND d.Location = 'New York');
```

EXISTS stops execution as soon as a match is found, improving performance.

5.3 Recursive CTEs for Hierarchical Data

A **recursive CTE** is useful for processing hierarchical data like **organizational charts** or **category trees**.

5.3.1 Basic Recursive CTE Example (Employee Hierarchy)

```
WITH EmployeeHierarchy AS (
    SELECT EmployeeID, EmployeeName, ManagerID, 1 AS HierarchyLevel
    FROM Employees
    WHERE ManagerID IS NULL   -- Start with top-level managers
    UNION ALL
    SELECT e.EmployeeID, e.EmployeeName, e.ManagerID,
eh.HierarchyLevel + 1
    FROM Employees e
    JOIN EmployeeHierarchy eh ON e.ManagerID = eh.EmployeeID
)
SELECT * FROM EmployeeHierarchy
ORDER BY HierarchyLevel, EmployeeID;
```

- Starts with employees who **don't have a manager** (top level).
- Recursively finds employees **reporting to managers** at the next level.

5.3.2 Recursive CTE for Category Tree

```
WITH CategoryTree AS (
    SELECT CategoryID, CategoryName, ParentCategoryID, 1 AS Level
    FROM Categories
    WHERE ParentCategoryID IS NULL
    UNION ALL
    SELECT c.CategoryID, c.CategoryName, c.ParentCategoryID, ct.Level
+ 1
    FROM Categories c
    JOIN CategoryTree ct ON c.ParentCategoryID = ct.CategoryID
)
SELECT * FROM CategoryTree
ORDER BY Level, CategoryID;
```

Useful for representing **nested product categories.**

5.4 When to Use CTEs vs. Temporary Tables

5.4.1 Using CTEs When Query is Read-Only and Used Inline

CTEs work best for:

- Breaking down **complex queries** into readable parts.
- **Recursive queries**.
- When you **don't need indexing** on the result set.

Example:

```
WITH HighSalaryEmployees AS (
    SELECT EmployeeID, EmployeeName, Salary
    FROM Employees
    WHERE Salary > 80000
)
SELECT * FROM HighSalaryEmployees;
```

5.4.2 Using Temporary Tables When Performance Matters

Temporary tables are better when:

- The data **needs indexing** for optimization.

- The result set is **used multiple times** in a session.

Example:

```
CREATE TABLE #HighSalaryEmployees (
    EmployeeID INT PRIMARY KEY,
    EmployeeName VARCHAR(100),
    Salary DECIMAL(10,2)
);

INSERT INTO #HighSalaryEmployees
SELECT EmployeeID, EmployeeName, Salary
FROM Employees
WHERE Salary > 80000;

SELECT * FROM #HighSalaryEmployees;
```

The **temporary table persists** for the session and can be indexed.

5.5 Summary

- **Optimize correlated subqueries** by replacing them with **JOINs** where possible.

- **Use recursive CTEs** for hierarchical data like **employee reporting structures and category trees**.

- **CTEs are best for readability and recursion**, while **temporary tables are better for performance** when indexing is needed.

Chapter 6: Dynamic SQL and Parameterized Queries

6.1 Introduction to Dynamic SQL

Dynamic SQL allows you to construct and execute SQL statements **at runtime**, making queries more flexible. However, improper usage can introduce **SQL injection vulnerabilities** and performance issues.

6.2 Writing Flexible, Secure Dynamic SQL

6.2.1 Basic Dynamic SQL Using EXEC

The simplest way to execute dynamic SQL is through the EXEC command.

```
DECLARE @sql NVARCHAR(MAX);
SET @sql = 'SELECT * FROM Employees WHERE DepartmentID = 3';
EXEC(@sql);
```

This executes the SQL string dynamically.

Problem: SQL Injection Risk

If user input is directly concatenated, it creates a serious **security vulnerability**.

```
DECLARE @dept NVARCHAR(50) = '3; DROP TABLE Employees'; -- Malicious
input
DECLARE @sql NVARCHAR(MAX);
SET @sql = 'SELECT * FROM Employees WHERE DepartmentID = ' + @dept;
EXEC(@sql);   -- Dangerous!
```

If an attacker enters 3; DROP TABLE Employees, it executes both queries, **deleting the table!**

6.3 Avoiding SQL Injection Risks with Parameterized Queries

6.3.1 Using sp_executesql for Safe Execution

A safer alternative is sp_executesql, which allows parameterized dynamic queries.

```
DECLARE @sql NVARCHAR(MAX);
DECLARE @DeptID INT = 3;

SET @sql = N'SELECT * FROM Employees WHERE DepartmentID = @Dept';
EXEC sp_executesql @sql, N'@Dept INT', @DeptID;
```

This **prevents SQL injection** by treating @Dept as a parameter rather than raw text.

6.3.2 Parameterized Query Example with User Input

If taking input from a user, always use parameters.

Unsafe Dynamic Query

```
DECLARE @UserInput NVARCHAR(50) = 'HR';
DECLARE @sql NVARCHAR(MAX);
SET @sql = 'SELECT * FROM Employees WHERE Department = ''' +
@UserInput + '''';
EXEC(@sql);   -- Risky!
```

A user could enter: **HR' OR 1=1 --**, returning all rows.

Safe Parameterized Query

```
DECLARE @sql NVARCHAR(MAX);
DECLARE @Dept NVARCHAR(50) = 'HR';

SET @sql = N'SELECT * FROM Employees WHERE Department = @Dept';
EXEC sp_executesql @sql, N'@Dept NVARCHAR(50)', @Dept;
```

The input is now a **bound parameter**, preventing manipulation.

6.4 Using EXEC and sp_executesql Effectively

6.4.1 When to Use EXEC vs. sp_executesql

Method	Pros	Cons
EXEC(@sql)	Simple, quick for static queries	Prone to **SQL injection**, no parameters
sp_executesql	Safer with **parameters**, reusable	Slightly more complex to write

6.4.2 Dynamic WHERE Clause Construction

Dynamic SQL is useful when building flexible filters based on user input.

Example: Search Query with Multiple Filters

```
DECLARE @sql NVARCHAR(MAX) = 'SELECT * FROM Employees WHERE 1=1';
DECLARE @Dept NVARCHAR(50) = 'HR';
DECLARE @MinSalary INT = NULL;

IF @Dept IS NOT NULL
    SET @sql = @sql + ' AND Department = @Dept';

IF @MinSalary IS NOT NULL
    SET @sql = @sql + ' AND Salary >= @MinSalary';

EXEC sp_executesql @sql, N'@Dept NVARCHAR(50), @MinSalary INT', @Dept,
@MinSalary;
```

This builds the query dynamically, adding filters only when needed.

6.5 Performance Considerations for Dynamic SQL

6.5.1 Query Plan Reuse with sp_executesql

- sp_executesql helps **cache execution plans**, improving performance.

- EXEC generates a <u>new plan every time</u>, which can be inefficient.

```
-- sp_executesql (Better for caching)
DECLARE @sql NVARCHAR(MAX) = N'SELECT * FROM Employees WHERE
DepartmentID = @DeptID';
EXEC sp_executesql @sql, N'@DeptID INT', @DeptID;
```

6.5.2 Avoiding Performance Bottlenecks

- **Use parameters** to ensure SQL Server reuses execution plans.

- **Limit dynamic SQL usage** to cases where **flexibility is necessary**.

6.6 Summary

- **Dynamic SQL enables flexible queries**, but **must be secured** to prevent SQL injection.

- **Always prefer sp_executesql over EXEC** to use parameterized queries.

- **Query plan reuse** improves performance, making parameterization a best practice.

Chapter 7: Advanced Transactions and Concurrency Control

7.1 Introduction to Transactions and Concurrency Control

- A **transaction** is a unit of work that must be **fully completed** or **rolled back** if an error occurs.

- **Concurrency control** ensures that multiple transactions can run **simultaneously** without data corruption.

- Poor transaction management can lead to **deadlocks, blocking, and performance issues**.

7.2 Isolation Levels and Their Impact on Queries

7.2.1 Understanding SQL Server Isolation Levels

SQL Server supports **five isolation levels** to control how transactions interact.

Isolation Level	Dirty Reads	Non-Repeatable Reads	Phantom Reads	Use Case
READ UNCOMMITTED	✓ Allowed	✓ Allowed	✓ Allowed	Fastest but risky (reporting only)
READ COMMITTED	✗ No	✓ Allowed	✓ Allowed	Default in SQL Server
REPEATABLE READ	✗ No	✗ No	✓ Allowed	Prevents data changes during a transaction
SERIALIZABLE	✗ No	✗ No	✗ No	Strictest, locks full range of rows
SNAPSHOT	✗ No	✗ No	✗ No	Uses versioning instead of locks

7.2.2 Changing Isolation Levels

You can manually set an isolation level before running queries.

```
SET TRANSACTION ISOLATION LEVEL REPEATABLE READ;
BEGIN TRANSACTION;

SELECT * FROM Orders WHERE CustomerID = 5;

COMMIT;
```

Ensures the same Orders data is **not modified** by other transactions while running.

7.3 Deadlocks, Blocking, and How to Troubleshoot Them

7.3.1 What Causes Deadlocks?

A **deadlock** happens when two transactions hold resources the other needs, creating a circular wait.

Example of a Deadlock

Transaction 1 (T1)

```
BEGIN TRANSACTION;
UPDATE Accounts SET Balance = Balance - 100 WHERE AccountID = 1;
WAITFOR DELAY '00:00:05';  -- Simulating delay
UPDATE Accounts SET Balance = Balance + 100 WHERE AccountID = 2;
COMMIT;
```

Transaction 2 (T2)

```
BEGIN TRANSACTION;
UPDATE Accounts SET Balance = Balance + 100 WHERE AccountID = 2;
WAITFOR DELAY '00:00:05';
UPDATE Accounts SET Balance = Balance - 100 WHERE AccountID = 1;
COMMIT;
```

- T1 locks **Account 1** and needs **Account 2**.

- T2 locks **Account 2** and needs **Account 1**.

- **Neither transaction can proceed, causing a deadlock.**

7.3.2 Detecting Deadlocks

SQL Server **automatically detects** deadlocks and kills **one of the transactions**. You can view deadlock details using **Extended Events** or **trace flags**.

Enable Deadlock Logging

```
ALTER DATABASE AdventureWorks SET ALLOW_SNAPSHOT_ISOLATION ON;
DBCC TRACEON (1222, -1); -- Enables deadlock tracking
```

View Deadlock Details

```
SELECT * FROM sys.dm_tran_locks;
SELECT * FROM sys.dm_exec_requests;
```

- **sys.dm_tran_locks** shows locked resources.

- **sys.dm_exec_requests** shows active queries.

7.3.3 Resolving Deadlocks

Solution 1: Ensure Consistent Lock Ordering

```
-- Always update AccountID 1 before AccountID 2 in all transactions
UPDATE Accounts SET Balance = Balance - 100 WHERE AccountID = 1;
UPDATE Accounts SET Balance = Balance + 100 WHERE AccountID = 2;
```

Ensures transactions access resources in **the same order**.

Solution 2: Reduce Lock Duration

```
SET TRANSACTION ISOLATION LEVEL READ COMMITTED;
BEGIN TRANSACTION;
UPDATE Accounts SET Balance = Balance - 100 WHERE AccountID = 1;
COMMIT;  -- Commit quickly to release locks
```

Commits **immediately** to free locks faster.

Solution 3: Use Snapshot Isolation

```
ALTER DATABASE AdventureWorks SET ALLOW_SNAPSHOT_ISOLATION ON;
SET TRANSACTION ISOLATION LEVEL SNAPSHOT;
```

Prevents blocking by using **row versioning** instead of locks.

7.4 Optimizing Queries in High-Concurrency Environments

7.4.1 Use Appropriate Indexing to Reduce Locking

Indexes **speed up queries** and **reduce contention** for concurrent transactions.

```
CREATE INDEX IX_Orders_CustomerID ON Orders (CustomerID);
```

Allows **faster lookups** without locking entire tables.

7.4.2 Minimize Locking with NOLOCK (Read Uncommitted Data **Carefully**)

For read-heavy workloads, NOLOCK can improve performance but **allows dirty reads**.

```
SELECT * FROM Orders WITH (NOLOCK) WHERE CustomerID = 5;
```

Best for reporting queries, but **should not be used for financial transactions**.

7.4.3 Use Optimistic Concurrency Control

For **frequent updates**, use **row versioning** instead of locking.

Example: Optimistic Concurrency Check

```
UPDATE Employees
SET Salary = 70000
WHERE EmployeeID = 1 AND LastUpdated = '2024-02-15 10:30:00';
```

Updates only if LastUpdated matches, preventing **stale updates**.

7.5 Summary

- **Choose the right isolation level** based on performance and consistency needs.
- **Deadlocks occur when transactions wait for each other's locks**—resolve by ensuring **consistent locking order** and **reducing transaction duration**.
- **Use indexing, NOLOCK for read-heavy workloads, and row versioning** to improve concurrency.

Chapter 8: Leveraging Temporary Tables, Table Variables, and Derived Tables

8.1 Introduction

When dealing with complex queries in SQL Server, understanding the right temporary data structure to use can significantly impact performance and maintainability. This chapter explores **temporary tables, table variables, and derived tables**, detailing when and how to use each efficiently.

8.2 When to Use Temp Tables vs. Table Variables

8.2.1 Temporary Tables (#TempTable)

Temporary tables are similar to permanent tables but exist only within a session. They are stored in tempdb and support indexing, statistics, and transactions.

Example: Creating and Using a Temporary Table

```
CREATE TABLE #SalesTemp (
    OrderID INT PRIMARY KEY,
    CustomerID INT,
    OrderTotal DECIMAL(10,2)
);

INSERT INTO #SalesTemp (OrderID, CustomerID, OrderTotal)
SELECT OrderID, CustomerID, SUM(TotalAmount)
FROM Sales
GROUP BY OrderID, CustomerID;

SELECT * FROM #SalesTemp;
DROP TABLE #SalesTemp;
```

Best Use Cases:

- Large datasets that need indexes for performance.
- Queries that require multiple reads/writes within a session.
- When transaction support is necessary.

8.2.2 Table Variables (@TableVar)

Table variables are stored in memory (though they may spill to tempdb) and exist only within the scope of a batch, function, or stored procedure. They don't support non-clustered indexes (except for primary keys).

Example: Using a Table Variable

```
DECLARE @SalesVar TABLE (
    OrderID INT PRIMARY KEY,
    CustomerID INT,
    OrderTotal DECIMAL(10,2)
);

INSERT INTO @SalesVar (OrderID, CustomerID, OrderTotal)
SELECT OrderID, CustomerID, SUM(TotalAmount)
FROM Sales
GROUP BY OrderID, CustomerID;

SELECT * FROM @SalesVar;
```

Best Use Cases:

- Small datasets that don't require indexing.

- When minimal logging is needed.

- In stored procedures where recompilation should be minimized.

8.2.3 Key Differences and When to Use Each

Feature	Temporary Table (#TempTable)	Table Variable (@TableVar)
Stored In	tempdb	Mostly memory (tempdb if needed)
Indexing Support	Yes	Limited (only PK)
Transaction Support	Yes	No
Scope	Session-wide	Batch-wide
Statistics Available	Yes	No (may affect performance in large queries)
Performance Impact	Can be optimized with indexes	Can perform poorly on large datasets

8.3 Performance Considerations of Temporary Objects

8.3.1 Temporary Table Performance Tips

- Index temporary tables if they are queried multiple times.
- Drop temporary tables when done (DROP TABLE #TempTable).
- Use SELECT INTO for large inserts (faster than INSERT INTO).

Example: Indexed Temp Table for Performance

```
CREATE TABLE #CustomerOrders (
    CustomerID INT,
    OrderTotal DECIMAL(10,2),
    INDEX IX_CustomerID CLUSTERED (CustomerID)
);
```

8.3.2 Table Variable Performance Tips

- Avoid using table variables for large datasets.
- Use primary keys for performance where applicable.

Example: Using a Primary Key in a Table Variable

```
DECLARE @CustomerSales TABLE (
    CustomerID INT PRIMARY KEY,
    TotalSales DECIMAL(10,2)
);
```

8.3.3 When to Use Derived Tables Instead

Derived tables (also known as **subqueries in the FROM clause**) are useful when data transformation is needed without explicitly creating a temporary structure.

8.4 Using Derived Tables for Complex Queries

8.4.1 What Are Derived Tables?

A **derived table** is a subquery used within the FROM clause that behaves like a table. It helps simplify complex joins and aggregations without requiring explicit temporary storage.

Example: Using a Derived Table for Aggregation

```
SELECT c.CustomerID, c.CustomerName, SalesSummary.TotalAmount
FROM Customers c
JOIN (
    SELECT CustomerID, SUM(OrderTotal) AS TotalAmount
    FROM Orders
    GROUP BY CustomerID
) SalesSummary ON c.CustomerID = SalesSummary.CustomerID;
```

Advantages:

- No need to explicitly create and drop a table.

- Can improve readability by simplifying queries.

- Works well when the derived table doesn't need indexes.

8.4.2 Combining Derived Tables with Joins

Derived tables are useful for breaking down complex queries into manageable parts.

Example: Nested Derived Tables for Customer Sales Ranking

```
SELECT CustomerID, CustomerName, TotalAmount, RANK() OVER (ORDER BY
TotalAmount DESC) AS SalesRank
FROM (
    SELECT c.CustomerID, c.CustomerName, SUM(o.OrderTotal) AS
TotalAmount
    FROM Customers c
    JOIN Orders o ON c.CustomerID = o.CustomerID
    GROUP BY c.CustomerID, c.CustomerName
) SalesData;
```

Key Benefits:

- Reduces the number of individual queries.

- Improves query organization and readability.

- Optimized by SQL Server's query planner.

8.5 Summary

- **Use temporary tables** when dealing with large datasets, needing indexes, or requiring transactions.

- **Use table variables** when handling small datasets, inside stored procedures, or when avoiding recompilations.

- Use derived tables for one-time, inline queries that don't require explicit indexing.

Choosing the right technique is crucial for performance optimization and query efficiency.

Chapter 9: Query Profiling and Performance Tuning Techniques

9.1 Introduction

Efficient SQL queries are crucial for high-performing databases. This chapter focuses on profiling tools and tuning techniques in SQL Server to identify performance bottlenecks and optimize queries.

9.2 Using SQL Server Profiler and Extended Events

9.2.1 SQL Server Profiler Overview

SQL Server Profiler is a graphical tool that captures and analyzes SQL query execution in real time. It is useful for identifying slow queries, deadlocks, and excessive resource usage.

Example: Creating a Trace in SQL Server Profiler

1.   Open **SQL Server Profiler**.

2.   Click **File > New Trace**, then connect to the database.

3.   Choose **TSQL-Duration** to track long-running queries.

4.   Start the trace and observe query execution times.

Key Events to Capture:

-   SQL:BatchCompleted (query execution details).

-   RPC:Completed (stored procedure execution details).

-   Showplan XML (query execution plan).

9.2.2 Extended Events (XEvents)

Extended Events (XEvents) provide a lightweight, high-performance alternative to SQL Server Profiler.

Example: Creating an Extended Event Session to Capture Slow Queries

```
CREATE EVENT SESSION SlowQueries ON SERVER
ADD EVENT sqlserver.sql_statement_completed (
    WHERE duration > 5000 -- Captures queries taking more than 5
seconds
)
ADD TARGET package0.event_file (SET
filename='C:\XEvents\SlowQueries.xel');
ALTER EVENT SESSION SlowQueries ON SERVER STATE = START;
```

- View captured events in **SQL Server Management Studio (SSMS)** under Extended Events.

- Stop the session when done:

- ALTER EVENT SESSION SlowQueries ON SERVER STATE = STOP;

Profiler vs. Extended Events:

Feature	SQL Server Profiler	Extended Events
Performance Impact	High	Low
GUI Available	Yes	Yes (SSMS)
Use for Production	No	Yes
Custom Filtering	Limited	Extensive

9.3 Analyzing Query Execution Statistics

9.3.1 Using Execution Plans

Execution plans help understand how SQL Server executes queries. There are two types:

- **Estimated Execution Plan:** Shows the plan without running the query.

- **Actual Execution Plan:** Includes runtime statistics.

Example: Viewing an Execution Plan in SSMS

1. Run the query with execution plan enabled:

2. SET SHOWPLAN_XML ON;

3. SELECT * FROM Orders WHERE OrderDate > '2023-01-01';

4. SET SHOWPLAN_XML OFF;

5. Alternatively, click **"Include Actual Execution Plan"** in SSMS and run the query.

Key Metrics in Execution Plans:

- **Clustered Index Seek:** Optimal operation, efficiently retrieves data.

- **Clustered Index Scan:** Reads the entire index, often inefficient.

- **Table Scan:** Reads the whole table, should be optimized with indexes.

- **Sort & Hash Match:** May indicate missing indexes or inefficient joins.

9.3.2 Using STATISTICS IO and STATISTICS TIME

These commands provide detailed query performance metrics.

Example: Measuring Query Performance

```
SET STATISTICS IO ON;
SET STATISTICS TIME ON;

SELECT CustomerID, SUM(OrderTotal)
FROM Orders
GROUP BY CustomerID;

SET STATISTICS IO OFF;
SET STATISTICS TIME OFF;
```

- **Logical Reads**: Number of pages read from memory.
- **Physical Reads**: Number of disk reads (should be minimized).
- **CPU Time**: Execution time in milliseconds.

9.4 Tuning Queries with Database Engine Tuning Advisor (DTA)

9.4.1 Introduction to Database Engine Tuning Advisor

DTA analyzes workload queries and suggests indexing strategies, partitioning, and statistics updates.

Steps to Use DTA in SSMS:

1. Open **Database Engine Tuning Advisor**.
2. Create a new session and load a query workload.
3. Click **"Start Analysis"** and review recommendations.
4. Apply suggested indexes using provided scripts.

9.4.2 Index Optimization

Indexes speed up query execution by reducing the need for full table scans.

Example: Creating an Index for Faster Query Performance

```
CREATE INDEX IX_Orders_CustomerID ON Orders(CustomerID);
```
- **Clustered Index:** Best for primary keys (PRIMARY KEY constraint).

- **Non-Clustered Index:** Useful for frequently queried columns.

9.4.3 Optimizing Joins and Subqueries

Example: Using Indexed Joins Instead of Scans

Without an index:

```
SELECT c.CustomerName, o.OrderTotal
FROM Customers c
JOIN Orders o ON c.CustomerID = o.CustomerID;
With an index on Orders.CustomerID:
CREATE INDEX IX_Orders_CustomerID ON Orders(CustomerID);
```

This reduces the need for a **hash join**, improving performance.

9.4.4 Using Query Hints for Fine-Tuning

Query hints allow manual optimization of execution plans.

Example: Forcing an Index Use

```
SELECT * FROM Orders WITH (INDEX(IX_Orders_CustomerID)) WHERE
CustomerID = 101;
```

- Use OPTION (RECOMPILE) to force query optimization each run.
- Use FORCESEEK to enforce an index seek.

9.5 Summary

- **SQL Server Profiler** and **Extended Events** help track slow queries.
- **Execution plans** and STATISTICS IO/TIME provide insights into query performance.
- **DTA** recommends indexes and optimizations.
- **Indexes, optimized joins, and query hints** improve performance.

Mastering these techniques ensures efficient SQL Server performance tuning.

Chapter 10: Best Practices for Writing Scalable SQL Queries

10.1 Introduction

Writing scalable SQL queries is essential for ensuring performance and maintainability as data volume grows. This chapter covers best practices for avoiding common pitfalls, structuring queries for readability, and optimizing them for future scalability.

10.2 Avoiding Common Anti-Patterns in Queries

10.2.1 Minimizing Functions in WHERE Clauses

Using functions on indexed columns prevents SQL Server from using indexes efficiently.

Example: Bad Query (Function on Indexed Column)

```sql
SELECT * FROM Orders WHERE YEAR(OrderDate) = 2023;
```

Optimized Query (Avoiding Functions in WHERE)

```sql
SELECT * FROM Orders WHERE OrderDate >= '2023-01-01' AND OrderDate < '2024-01-01';
```

Why?

- Allows SQL Server to use an index on OrderDate.
- Reduces full table scans.

10.2.2 Avoiding Unnecessary Joins

Excessive or redundant joins can slow down queries.

Example: Bad Query (Unnecessary Joins)

```sql
SELECT c.CustomerID, c.CustomerName, o.OrderTotal
FROM Customers c
LEFT JOIN Orders o ON c.CustomerID = o.CustomerID
LEFT JOIN OrderDetails od ON o.OrderID = od.OrderID;
```

Optimized Query (Removing Redundant Joins)

```sql
SELECT CustomerID, CustomerName FROM Customers;
```

Why?

- Avoids bringing in data that isn't needed.

- Improves execution speed by reducing the complexity of the query.

10.2.3 Using EXISTS Instead of IN for Subqueries

IN is less efficient for large datasets compared to EXISTS.

Example: Bad Query (Using IN)

```
SELECT * FROM Customers WHERE CustomerID IN (SELECT CustomerID FROM
Orders);
```

Optimized Query (Using EXISTS)

```
SELECT * FROM Customers c WHERE EXISTS (SELECT 1 FROM Orders o WHERE
o.CustomerID = c.CustomerID);
```

Why?

EXISTS stops checking once a match is found, making it faster than IN.

10.3 Structuring Queries for Maintainability and Readability

10.3.1 Using CTEs (Common Table Expressions) for Complex Queries

CTEs improve query readability and break down complex queries into logical steps.

Example: Using a CTE for Better Readability

```
WITH OrderTotals AS (
    SELECT CustomerID, SUM(OrderTotal) AS TotalSpent
    FROM Orders
    GROUP BY CustomerID
)
SELECT c.CustomerID, c.CustomerName, ot.TotalSpent
FROM Customers c
JOIN OrderTotals ot ON c.CustomerID = ot.CustomerID;
```

Why?

- Makes queries more structured and easier to debug.

- Reusable within the query.

10.3.2 Using Meaningful Aliases

Use clear and concise aliases to improve query readability.

Example: Bad Query (Unclear Aliases)

```
SELECT c.CustomerID, c.CustomerName, o.OrderID, o.OrderTotal
FROM Customers c
JOIN Orders o ON c.CustomerID = o.CustomerID
JOIN OrderDetails od ON o.OrderID = od.OrderID;
```

Optimized Query (Descriptive Aliases)

```
SELECT cust.CustomerID, cust.CustomerName, ord.OrderID, ord.OrderTotal
FROM Customers AS cust
JOIN Orders AS ord ON cust.CustomerID = ord.CustomerID
JOIN OrderDetails AS odet ON ord.OrderID = odet.OrderID;
```

Why?

Improves readability and maintainability.

10.3.3 Formatting Queries for Readability

Proper indentation and line breaks make queries easier to read.

Example: Well-Formatted Query

```
SELECT
    c.CustomerID,
    c.CustomerName,
    SUM(o.OrderTotal) AS TotalSpent
FROM Customers AS c
JOIN Orders AS o ON c.CustomerID = o.CustomerID
GROUP BY c.CustomerID, c.CustomerName
HAVING SUM(o.OrderTotal) > 1000
ORDER BY TotalSpent DESC;
```

Why?

- Easier to read and maintain.
- Clear separation of clauses.

10.4 Future-Proofing Queries for Large-Scale Data Growth

10.4.1 Using Proper Indexing

Indexes improve query speed, especially as data grows.

Example: Creating an Index for Faster Lookups

```
CREATE INDEX IX_Orders_CustomerID ON Orders(CustomerID);
```

Why?

Reduces table scans and improves filtering performance.

10.4.2 Partitioning Large Tables

Partitioning helps manage large datasets by dividing them into smaller, manageable chunks.

Example: Partitioning by Order Date

```
CREATE PARTITION FUNCTION OrderDatePartition (DATE)
AS RANGE LEFT FOR VALUES ('2022-12-31', '2023-12-31', '2024-12-31');
```

Why?

Improves query performance by reducing the number of scanned rows.

10.4.3 Optimizing Pagination for Large Result Sets

Pagination should be optimized to avoid performance issues with large data sets.

Example: Bad Pagination (Using OFFSET Without Indexing)

```
SELECT * FROM Orders ORDER BY OrderDate OFFSET 50000 ROWS FETCH NEXT
100 ROWS ONLY;
```

Optimized Pagination (Using an Indexed Column for Pagination)

```
SELECT * FROM Orders WHERE OrderID > 50000 ORDER BY OrderID FETCH NEXT
100 ROWS ONLY;
```

Why?

- Avoids scanning all previous rows.

- Uses indexing efficiently.

10.4.4 Avoiding Deadlocks with Proper Query Ordering

Deadlocks occur when multiple queries lock resources in a conflicting order.

Example: Standardizing Lock Order to Prevent Deadlocks

```
BEGIN TRANSACTION;

UPDATE Customers SET CustomerName = 'John Doe' WHERE CustomerID = 1;
UPDATE Orders SET OrderTotal = 500 WHERE CustomerID = 1;

COMMIT TRANSACTION;
```

Why?

Ensures consistent locking order to avoid conflicts.

10.5 Summary

- **Avoid query anti-patterns** like functions in WHERE clauses.

- **Use CTEs, formatting, and meaningful aliases** for readability.

- **Future-proof queries** with indexing, partitioning, and optimized pagination.

- **Prevent deadlocks** by maintaining consistent lock order.

By following these best practices, SQL queries remain **efficient, maintainable, and scalable** as data grows.

Chapter 11: Conclusion - Advancing SQL Expertise for Real-World Performance

Mastering SQL is not just about writing queries—it's about crafting solutions that are **efficient, scalable, and maintainable**. This book has provided a structured approach to **query optimization, indexing strategies, advanced joins, window functions, dynamic SQL, and performance tuning**, all aimed at empowering database professionals with expert-level skills.

Through real-world techniques, readers have learned to **analyze execution plans, leverage indexing for query acceleration, use window functions for advanced analytics, and implement optimized transaction handling for high-concurrency environments**. Additionally, **profiling and tuning techniques** have been covered to help diagnose and fix performance bottlenecks efficiently.

As databases grow in complexity, the principles in this book will serve as a **foundation for continuous learning and adaptation**. The SQL landscape is ever-evolving, with new challenges emerging as data volumes increase and business needs shift. By applying the strategies outlined here, SQL professionals can ensure their queries remain **fast, efficient, and future-proof**—no matter the scale.

This book is not just a reference but a **practical guide to becoming an SQL Server expert**. The journey doesn't end here—keep experimenting, refining, and optimizing queries to push the boundaries of SQL performance.